Sharing News

Cynthia Rothman

You have news.
How will you
share your news?

Will you tell someone
your news?

Will you call on the telephone
and tell someone your news?

Will you write your news
in a letter?

Will you send your news
by e-mail?

On the screen: Viewing Your E-Mail

Hi
GRANDPA
See You
SATURDAY
Love,
Ben

Will your news
be in a school report?

Will your news
be in a newspaper?

Will your news
be on the radio?

Will your news
be on television?

How We Share News

by telephone

on television

by telling

on the radio

in a newspaper

by e-mail

in a report

in a letter

He has news.
How will he share it?